The Defying GENTRIFICATION Playbook:

A Memoir + Manifesto for Black Queer Feminist Disabled Urbanism

Kristen E. Jeffers

THE BLACK URBANIST

Copyright 2025, Kristen E. Jeffers

Kristen Jeffers Media

Paperbackt ISBN: 9781733456210

Hardcover ISBN 9781733456234

EPUB ISBN: 9781733456227

Audio ISBN: 9781733456203

All images copyright or courtesy of Kristen Jeffers

Designed and typeset by Kristen Jeffers

Learn more about Defying Gentrification and Kristen's work at www.defyinggentrification.com

Table of CONTENTS

The Defying Gentrification Manifesto	**6**
How To Use This Book	**8**
Prologue: Why DEFY Gentrification	**14**
Introduction: My Journey to Defying Gentrification	**22**
Part 1: The Things I Can Do	**36**
I can have faith	**38**
I can create and cultivate	**44**
I can care for myself	**52**
Part 2: What I Need From You.	**64**
I need community care	**66**
I need infrastructure	**74**
I need access	**80**
I need convenience	**86**
Part 3: The Work (Book) We All Need To Do	**92**
Conclusion: What's Next	**108**
Acknowledgments	**113**

Defying GENTRIFICATION Manifesto

I can have **faith**, I can **create** and **cultivate**, and **care for myself**, but I need **community care, infrastructure, access, and convenience** from others to **DEFY GENTRIFICATION**.

How to Use This Book

I wrote this book to give myself a book of urbanism that I could read for motivation, use in formal and informal community engagement activities, and help me navigate personal urbanist realities.

Sad realities like being in the process of eviction. Happy realities, as insisting that I find someone to make my afro-curly hair rainbow-colored.

I also wrote myself a manifesto, which you saw when you opened the book, to guide me. Sometimes, I even say it out loud as an affirmation. Other times, I print it and post it around town. Maybe that's how you found this book. Welcome, this is where I tell you what that manifesto you saw is all about.

I would often look around in the rooms I was in, especially the first ten years of my work, writing my blog, The Black Urbanist, and I would be the only Black person. And let's not get into how Blackness is not nearly the monolith that whiteness wants to be and wants to force on us.

I also grew up in one church, one of hate, and now, I've built a cornucopia of spirituality, that, while contains some elements of my childhood faith, invites me to remember that I am enough, I have a reason for being here, and that my environment is sacred and I want to do my part to make it that way. Hence, my love of and need for a mantra, both written and audible, to make my way in life.

With that being said, for many of you, this will be a book to read from start to finish, stopping to do the workbook chapters.

However, if you and I share almost all of the same identities and cultures, stop reading after the chapter on self-care in part one and skip ahead to part three on doing the work, so that you can craft your plan of self-care, faith, creativity, and cultivation.

We are often tasked with doing the community care, creating the access, making things convenient, and building the infrastructure, even if we are penniless, gravely ill, or a color that will get us arrested or deported.

Sisters, and other gender-expansive folks who rock like this, I know you can do it. But what I want you to ask yourself, in the context of pushing against the things gentrification brings to us on the daily, do you need to do it?

And if so, how can you find the people to help you? How can you accept help? How can you find help that's not just well-meaning, but well-doing and well-being?

If you do decide to read part two, please do not obligate yourself to do that work, outside of making sure you decolonize yourself so you can properly do the community care from a healed and grounded place. Use the workbook sections to ask those who are going to be reading part two and needing to do the work to make sure parts one and two happen for you, to help you, and to shape that work for yourself.

For everyone else, even if you have a small degree of marginalization, please read the whole thing. Then, when you get to the workbook section, those questions I ask you on solidarity and facilitating belonging, access, and justice are the questions you should focus on when it comes to shaping an ideal environment free of gentrification.

Depending on where you sit on the scales of marginalization and in the systems of privilege in society, you may get some value out of the first section, especially the ones on faith and creativity.

However, your self-care should not come at the disadvantage of folks like me.

To my Black brothers, time is up for sisters to feed you your plate first. Oh, and when you start talking about buying back the block, remember to make sure the beauty salon gets to stay, and the sisters don't have to hear you getting slick at the mouth about their bodies without asking first.

For my white folks, time is up for your peace and light-only yoga studio or your bro-time barber and bourbon shop to willingly or indirectly push out the African dance studio or Black hair shop that provides affirmation that our movements and our crowns aren't abominations.

For my siblings in the global majority who don't have Africa in their family history, your food isn't more exotic than ours, and I need you to stop being the agent of our joint oppressor by claiming we don't want to create community spaces. Sometimes, the white developer only sees value in you and sees value in your labor. Not you, and if your food gets too nasty or spicy, they'll throw you away, too.

Finally, in an ableist world, our abilities will be constricted, but we can get started being more inclusive by demanding wider doors, quieter rooms, faster elevators, pristine air quality, and beyond equal access to healthcare we need.

We can also pray, meditate, or just do good deeds together, but if you think my transness and queerness are hellbound, low vibration, or disruptive to the best order of society, fuck that shit.

Oh, I forgot to tell you, this book has strategically placed curse words. These are mainly in areas where I want to express true low vibrational and hellish behavior in order for us to get rid of the false ideas that it's ok to turn places into hellscapes and that hellscapes are permanent and unrelenting.

They aren't, just like gentrification isn't inevitable.

Because this is a workbook that touches on sensitive areas, you may cry and rage. But what I ask you to do is not run away from that feeling and do at least one thing daily to help you get past those feelings and create solutions around them that are affirming and freeing.

Also, don't try to do this all in one sitting. Use those grounding practices, because even though self-care doesn't look the same for all of us, grounding often does, because grounding comes from our best selves.

So, now that we've established how I see you using this book, let's go.

Prologue: Why DEFY GENTRIFICATION

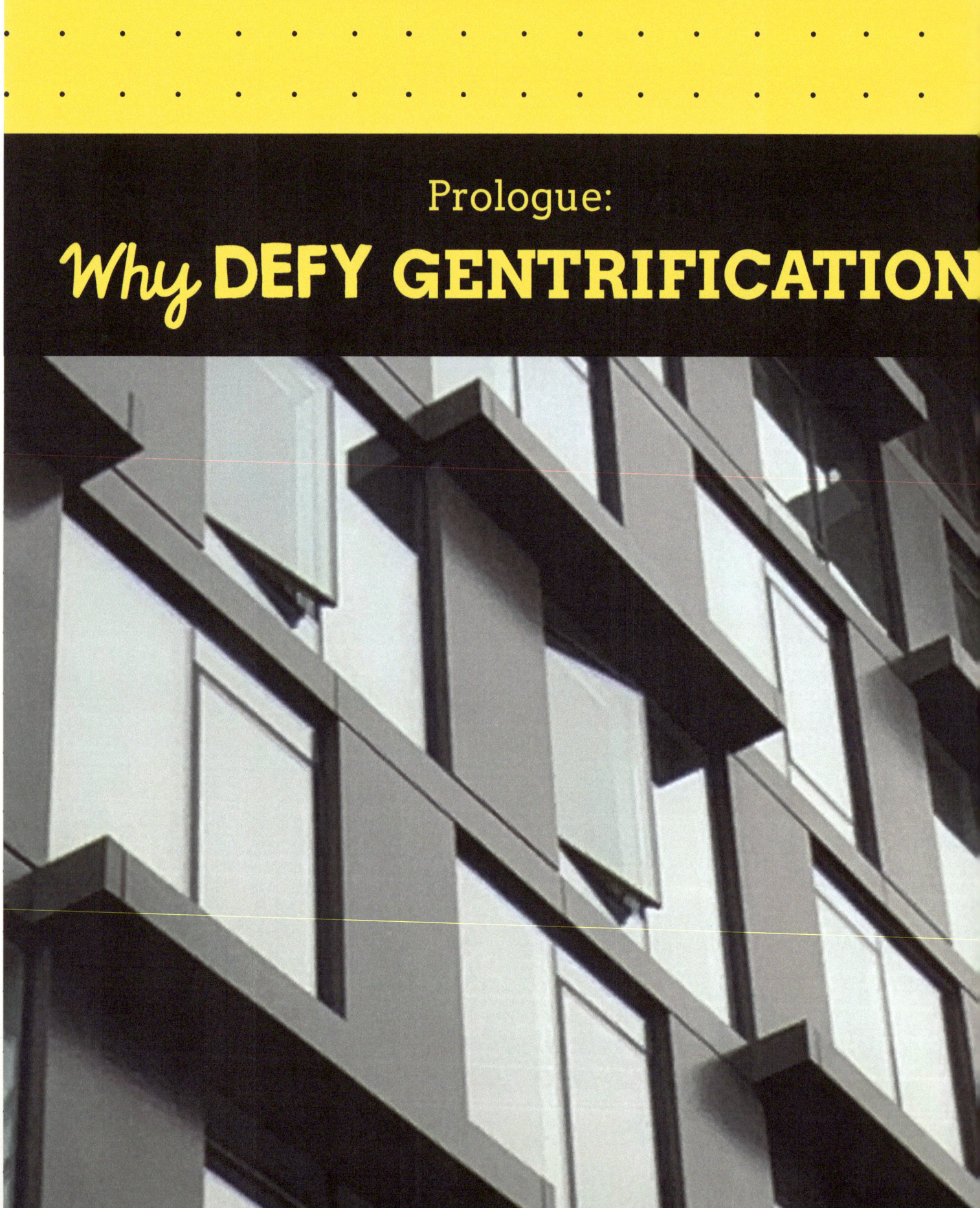

Don't you get tired of waking up every morning and proving that you deserve to exist? Even if you're not actively being ethnically cleansed or harassed or doxxed, it gets annoying to get up every morning and tell the world, Hello, I'm a human. These are my reasons to exist.

As an underpaid Black queer, autistic cultural and urban planning worker and professional artist, gentrification makes me feel I'm subhuman.

Why?

Let's start by explaining the roots of the word and concept of gentrification.
The concept of gentrification was first introduced by white British sociologist Ruth Glass in 1964 in the introduction to her book London: Aspects of Change. In it, she spoke of the idea of replacing one set of people (in this case, poor people) with wealthier people, in cities, through everything from direct evictions to raising rents or taxes such that pressure is put on people who can no longer afford to stay where they are, to find somewhere else to live.

The people being replaced in the neighborhood Glass was analyzing were Black folks from the Caribbean and other African countries in the British Commonwealth. The people replacing them were white artists and bohemians, who loved the Black culture, but the posh white landlords loved that their own children and grandchildren with white skin were returning to their old neighborhoods.
Because yes, only in a few cases, have American neighborhoods that are desirable and humane, have been built specifically for people of African decent first. We generally get the neighborhoods after someone else has used them or someone, usually of European decent, has taken the lands from us, deemed them undesirable for them and then, drawn up both physical and on paper borders for where we are desirable to live.

Everyone else from everywhere else is tokenized by white landowners and sadly, sometimes becomes a middleman of sorts between Black land equity. And then, when we do get the land, we often feel like it should be a business proposition, instead of being creative about keeping people housed. Or they're removed too, when the power structure says times up.

Some refuse to define gentrification in such a way. I can't afford not to, because like other sociological phenomena that have been observed in people of African descent, especially those of us who were descendants of the enslaved and the Jim Crow segregated, it's not just a theory, it's a way of life, often limiting and destructive.The gentrification apologists will also tell you that there's nothing wrong with developers and landlords replacing poor people with wealthier people.

That a building's value can climb up a rent and price scale of their own imagination, until buildings, otherwise capable, sturdy, necessary buildings of shelter, retail, education, spiritual relief, and other community gathering spaces sit empty.

That lands can lie fallow, crop-less, and purposeless for years.

That some people deserve to be rich and make enough either through their own labor or exploitation of other people's labor, to pay for things at ever higher prices.

Lands in limbo as the vegetation and the reclamation of the Earth that nature does to itself when it has been clear-cut, is not allowed to happen, because there's always the higher bidder, and the right price.

But in this book, I'll be coming from my perspective as a US-born and raised descendant of enslaved Africans and Jim Crow segregated Negros who made themselves Black and Proud, in what's been called North Carolina since colonization. I'm also pansexual and nonbinary agender, but I tend to be perceived as a straight, lighter-skinned, white-adjacent/safe (thank you loose curls) nerdy Black woman. Not long before I sent this to press, I was confirmed autistic, and I may have some elements of ADHD, but I've been depressed and anxious for years.

My strong sense of justice and big feelings, and love of aesthetics, have kept me from keeping a job longer than about 18 months, that's full-time and paid fairly.

The jobs I've had have been in nonprofits that emphasize the vow of poverty. People assume that, as a bookish person, I am great at details, but I'm better at color matching. Please forgive me for any typos you still find in this book.

I graduated with a degree in communication, with a public relations concentration, into the Research Triangle Park of 2008, where I was able to start a low-paying job supporting venture capitalists, and live in a nice apartment for decent rent nearby, but I was laid off just six months into the job.

And I'm sick of what gentrification has done to me and folks like me, some who can't even get in the rooms I do have access to because of my couple of privileges as a "model minority."

However, I don't think you have to be me to defy gentrification. In fact, when I see someone who has even more of what's been deemed by our capitalistic and imperialistic society as bad, manages to maintain shelter, and has shelter that provides for those they love, soothes themselves and also is friendly to our one Mother Earth, then all I can do is jump and down and scream all the YASSSSS-es in the world, because you made it.

I want to make it so that anybody can make it, and that gets me to why we are using a Black, queer, accessible, feminist, and urbanist framework and how we will go about doing so in this book.

I'll actually explain what I mean by that framework in the later part of the book. First, I'm going to share my journey to defying gentrification and I'm going to break down the Defying Gentrification Manifesto I started this book with:

I can have faith, I can create and cultivate, and care for myself, but I need community care, infrastructure, access, and convenience to defy gentrification.

Introduction:
My Journey to Defying GENTRIFICATION

It all started with a map.

My dad was a licensed electrician and had been for about six years before I was born. He'd only been doing it for about three years when he walked in on my mom in her junior high school classroom, I imagine, with her head in her hands, grading papers, to fix a fluorescent light that wouldn't stop flickering.

My dad's desire and love for my mom wouldn't stop flickering, and he came up with reasons to come into her room, and their conversations launched into dates, which not long after launched into marriage, then a journey to have me and to establish a home.

I was born on December 14, 1985, and a few months earlier, our new family home was established on Rockett Street in Greensboro, NC.

The maps that my dad brought me would not tell me that our home came with a residential covenant when it was built in 1949, banning people like us from ever possessing it, but of course, that was laughable considering that by 1985, the owners were happy to sell it to us, after a short rental period.

No, we weren't even on those maps, but those maps weren't needed for the prejudice to continue onward. And it was that kind of prejudice in payment and my mom's desire for me to be her only student for the earliest years of my life, that sent my dad out after his days doing maintenance at the school system, to what was then the Greensboro Daily News, and out to the various truck stops by our growing international airport, recently expanded.

He would drop off the papers, freshly off the presses, and sometimes in return, he would bring home the maps the truck stops would print, advertisements for them, helping their patrons know exactly where to go from where they'd stopped off for the night.

Those maps and a few extra ones ignited a passion in me when my dad would bring them home and place them next to the Chutes and Ladders board game that I would insist on playing as much as my parents had the space and time to play. I would draw and drive toy NASCARs on those maps, dreaming of going somewhere besides across town.

However, being an only child afforded me attention from my parents that many other children, even some who are in much better financial situations than we were, don't get. Actually, my parents loving the fact that they had a child, especially after having had some birth complications, made the difference.

My mom took joy in introducing me to the ins and outs of our local Harris Teeter and Food Lion grocery stores. I was apparently a hit at one of the Harris Teeters, where several of her former students couldn't get enough of Mrs. Jeffers's little girl to the point where I got to stand on the checkout counter. My mom would also shape my love of crafting, but more on that a little later.

My parents would be in our backyard, dad noodling on something around his shed, or taking me on house or church calls to fix lights all through the homes of worship and families of Black Greensboro. Mom would be working on her plants, or we would be headed to one of the New Garden nursery locations on the outskirts of town.

Or we would be on the actual outskirts of town or deep in the country, back in their roots as rural Black folks, sitting around tables of food with grandparents, siblings, and cousins, recounting old family stories and stuffing our bellies with things prepared by either my MeMe (my mom's mom) or my dad's siblings, who would always bring out every single dessert possible for our family reunions at Thanksgiving. Or, if it was the summer, my mom's extended family would gather us at Graham Park, around all the southern fish fried and burgers grilled, and a sand-filled playground that was a little odd so far inland from the ocean.

There were also street festivals and Friday night high school football games, and later on, two houses as my parents needed to live apart, but still wanted to co-parent and support me.

There were the various branches of the Greensboro Public Library, especially both the Benchmark and Southwest Branches, which would later merge into the Hemphill Branch, walking distance from my mom and I's first solo place, but long after we'd moved into the house that I started writing this book in. And of course, the Glenwood Branch, celebrating 30 years in 2023 of serving the community, and of course, having a special place in my heart as a young child who got to witness a brand new library opening.

I was a Borders Rewards member, but I reluctantly supported Barnes and Noble and BAM! (Books a Million), and am forever grateful to all the independent bookstores that have nurtured me as I've written this book and its predecessor.

I honestly thought that my public relations degree was going to be the prelude to me attending law school. Everyone else was doing political science and pre-law, and I thought that I would be different and do communication.

Truth be told, communication was my second-choice major at NC State University. Years prior, I had submitted a portfolio of my songs, with a very early 2000s photo-edited version of my drawing of some musical notes and staffs affixed to the cover of the workbook as my portfolio for my in-person design review.

This wouldn't have been an issue, but I was applying to graphic design school, not writing school, but thankfully, I got kicked over to writing school, and I loved it so much, I stayed, but never without being engaged in art and design and music, despite getting more involved in campus politics.

I also came to campus without a car and lived in a standard dorm for my 3.5 years there. However, my campus had its own very robust bus line, the Wolfline. It was free and open to anyone, as long as you were ok with going where it went. There were two Food Lions, a Kmart, a Cookout, and a Bojangles on the lines. Plus, we had access to what was then called the CAT, the Capital Area Transit buses, for free. That would take you downtown, to what was known as Cameron Village, even though it was closer to me in my dorms than some parts of our vast village of a campus, and the Crabtree Valley Mall.

We had amazing dining halls, sparkling convenience stores, and even our own sports "bar" and several national fast food chains. We also have an award-winning ice cream brand and stand on campus, the Howling Cow.

At the time, the Howling Cow Ice Cream stand inside of DH Hill, nor the Target that replaced Western Lanes, was operating. But still, I had Talley Taco Bell and so many resources at my disposal on foot.

Years later, I would write in a blog post that everything I learned about urbanism I learned on campus, and that's still true to this day.

Plus, when it came time to go to grad school, after getting a taste of the real world during the Great Recession, I chose the school that not only gave me a full scholarship, but also had a targeted, blended program in public administration, nonprofit management, and community and economic development.

It was sitting at UNC Greensboro in my first semester urban policy class, that I realized that I needed to re-write my textbook. And it wasn't enough to do it on a blog that only talked about these things part-time. The Black Urbanist was born.

For the next eight years, I would write, and then I would get invited to speak at various conferences. I would go into debt, even when I was working on some community projects that paid, but not often, and by invoice.

My Twitter ballooned and plateaued at around 14,000 followers.

I got staff jobs as a communication and public affairs and marketing coordinator at several nonprofits in every city I lived in, some full-time, others part-time and contract.

But in 2018, the biggest shift came no sooner than I had set foot back in DC in a new rented room after a year of couch surfing and Uber and Lyft driving in rented vehicles in between my nonprofit gig in Baltimore.

Honestly, this part of the story really starts back in 2016 on a Zoom. Yes, Zoom existed way back then, and no, people didn't mute themselves properly.

But because a certain participant of that Zoom didn't mute properly, a seed was planted in my heart and mind about something I thought I'd hidden about myself.

To hear my now wife Les tell the story, it started in 2014, when she was thinking about how so many people in the hood were privy to cigarettes. She then decided to Google the words Black and urbanism and my blog was number one.

I had written an article on my blog called Does it Matter Who Owns the Corner Store, and I had spoken not just of Black American elders, but of immigrants of color who I would later learn were assimilating into negative stereotypes of Black folks due to colonialism. I would speak of LGBTQIA+ people deserving to have a space in that corner store, while thinking that I wasn't one of them.

She told me later that seeing that in the article made her bookmark my page and start being a fan from afar.

However, I had repressed my bi-ness, partly because it was clear that it was not accepted. I asked out both a boy and a girl in middle school, and ran away from a gender-non-conforming classmate who tried to ask me out.

My hair had broken off seemingly overnight between sixth and seventh grade, and the shorter my hair got, the more I felt masculine, and the longer it was, the more feminine. However, not only was it not cool to have crushes on everyone in 1998, it wasn't cool to switch gender presentations, or even wear glasses then, either. Let's not start with having naturally curly and kinky hair. One of my teachers had looser curls as a white woman, and it was celebrated when she cut them down. Another teacher, also white, had skin that was deemed too pale, so logic wasn't the greatest at my middle school.

Don't let anyone convince you that the late 90s were progressive. Remind them that even though Ellen DeGeneres came out of the closet on TV, and Oprah was her therapist, off the screen, things were way more fraught.

So, I stuffed my crush on Natalie Imbruglia and several other lady celebrities of all races and gender presentations down, got louder about preferring the boys of *NSYNC over the Backstreet Boys and Immature over Boyz II Men, and got through all of my years of schooling, being conservative on the inside and outside.

When I started dating white men, as a child of North Carolina, it was my first taste of bringing home people that my family might have something to say about. It was also that second white man who connected Les and I on that Zoom call.

That night in 2016, on my mustard-colored couch in Kansas City, I brushed off my intrigue.

After all, I was too busy having a nervous breakdown at my job, from which my now ex was supposed to be my savior. Mind you, some of the white folks there made me wish I could take my lighter-than-a-paper-bag skin on and off, much like Max does with his monster suit in Where the Wild Things Are. Later, I would learn about how that book is a queer metaphor.

I asked my ex and he said it was ok to quit my job, come back east, start doing Kristen Jeffers Media and Design full-time, and we would move my stuff into his standard-issue 2010s gentrification-era DC apartment.

Two weeks after I quit said job, my ex told me he needed to quit me.

Yeah, didn't see that one coming, nor did I fully understand, despite being in therapy as a child of a bipolar father, just how deep my depression was.

But, I did notice I found joy not just in expressing myself in what's known in the queer subculture as a hard feminine way, but I also found joy in seeing women who looked like what I wanted to look like.

Those women, with bright colored hair and angled curls, that I saw on Pinterest, when I was doing the age-old emerging queer pastime, deciding on a more queer haircut to tell the world who I was, tickled that queer itch just perfectly.

Maybe I should expand out of my comfort zone and explore relationships with people who weren't cis men.

So I did. There was one actual human I had a fling with, but that was just it, a fling. I told all the queer urbanists I knew in and around DC and Baltimore, and no one seemed to freak out.

But it took me taking the initiative with Les, in the fall of 2018, after a date at the Midlands Beer Garden, to completely shift my worldview into Black queer feminist urbanism.

I noticed that she was experiencing the world differently.

We were in DC, but she was struggling at times to make ends meet, and she mentioned being cut out of pictures published in major newspapers, and asked not to represent her company at events.

She could navigate certain streets due to her masculine appearance. She would navigate unscathed, and I would get catcalled. She mentioned one time, though that a man did try to hit on her, revealing his flexibility in dating people of all kinds of gender presentations. Still, it was street harassment, and it was shitty and uncomfortable.

Whereas I felt most comfortable living in whiter neighborhoods, where I could only afford to rent rooms, she had a whole apartment in a neighborhood still considered the hood, though gentrification has raised its rents too over the course of the five years she'd lived there before me.

We spent five more years together in that apartment. When I moved in, in the spring of 2019, I felt so much shame that I, a person who had made a big show of selling my Honda Accord I'd had since I graduated college in the fall of 2007 and attempting a car-free life, needed to drive again.

However, Shanequa Annabelle, our 2016 Honda Fit that we purchased together in 2019 is a character in her own right, opening up the doors for me to see, much like I saw during my rental car years in Baltimore, just how spread out and pushed out communities of color and their special foodways and music and art and design and someone who could do my hair without an odd fascination, were in the so-called Chocolate City and its Vanilla suburbs.

By the end of 2019, after living in utter fear that my queerness would be a liability, despite doing a "hometown tour" of keynote speeches across North Carolina with Les by my side, I was starting to feel confident that things would be ok.

But after one more psychotic break and a terrible, week-long cold at what would be my last time working in an office five days a week, trying to be a nonprofit communication assistant, a mysterious novel coronavirus, would forever change all of our lives.

In the early days of the middle-class office employee lockdowns, I used my skills of negotiation to get Les a doctor's note to stay home. Her office then claimed they were medically necessary and therefore, she needed to work in the office. For several months, said office acted like they couldn't use virtual timesheets, then they finally learned how to do that. Les also got promoted, then unpromoted.

She had had a fibroid procedure right when we locked down, and we had been in quarantine together anyway. We basically did that for the better part of the last five years.

I managed to do some virtual talks, but one night, on the day of my Dad's death anniversary in May 2025, the world started mourning George Floyd. Yet another Black man snuffed out by police on camera for the world to see.

I immediately felt irrelevant. I couldn't stay up all night, and that seemed to be what was required for me to succeed as a diversity consultant in these new times.

I tried to have my own Black queer feminist urbanist conference with mitigations in the fall of 2021. I taught a course in Black queer feminist urbanism, but then pulled back because I felt like I was just bitter and something was missing.

We got vaccinated, and Les's lungs started collapsing again.

Les started her nonprofit, endoQueer, to make sense of all these things going on with her body and assert that her body and others like it deserve adequate health care at all times.

I started crocheting more. This started because I found a new hairdresser who took safety precautions and realized I should be wearing satin bonnets, but I still wanted them to look more like crocheted berets. I even dyed my hair blue and purple. Now we're in the rainbow fro era, nearly five years later as of this writing.

And then, I learned about disability justice. As the world tried to open back up, we found ourselves still needing to mask, I needing to have my own fibroids removed, and just six months prior to me writing these words, my nerves went into overdrive and my back pain and weight increased. Oh, and I think this book wouldn't let me finish it until I started the process of my AuDHD diagnosis, but it's in progress and it's the entire bow on top of everything I've ever gone through.

I took 2024 completely off after getting COVID and having more panic attacks. And I've barely blogged. But one morning in 2025, the morning I'm editing these words, everything locked in and…

So here we are.

This workbook is a journey for you to find what you need, because it contains the tools I used to do just that.

I hope to be able to train you, in person or from afar, to figure out what it is that people like me need to succeed in cities. And what you need to succeed for yourself.

In the first section, I identify three things people who share identity markers with me need to defy gentrification, despite everything thrown at us. Then, in the middle are the worksheets that drill down into the finances, mindsets, affirmations, and reference materials you need to succeed.

Then, in the later part of the workbook, I call on our allies to provide four things to help us in our quest, and I encourage everyone to think of people not as burdens or consumers, but fellow stewards of the Earth.

Now that we've set the stage for this journey, let's get started!

Part 1:
The Things I Can Do

Thing I Can Do 1:
I can have faith

When you hear the word faith, I know what you're thinking. Stained glass. Wooden pews. An organ. Black church elders singing one of those moaning and groaning songs that only have five words, but somehow it manages to last an hour.

Or half of it is someone's testimony that you know piece by piece. And depending on what church, maybe it's the elders trying to moan in Latin or interpret some other tongues.

I know we want to laugh at our elders sometimes, but when they were singing those songs and shouting and telling the same story over and over again, they were on to something.

If they were sitting in a church they put their extremely hard-earned money together to buy, they might have been tarrying and moaning in prayer to the Lord to make sure that it stayed in their hands and the graveyards were honored and respected.

Somebody knew somebody, especially if that somebody was the person that they saw in the mirror, who had lost the house that they had built.

Mind you, the house was built as a slave cabin, then added on to over the 40 years of sharecropping that happened, but your aunt got a scholarship to college and now she's a lawyer who managed not to lose her whole mind working for that big-time, white man-led law firm up North. But she couldn't get your uncles and your dad on the same page, and your grandparents died without a will.

Meanwhile, on the next pew, your 95-year-old neighbor is excited that her children are gathering safely for the first time since the pandemic, at her house, and they all met and decided who was going to inherit and be able to profit.

They recognized that their parents had pulled off a small miracle by scraping together the money from various maid, restaurant, and factory jobs in the segregated South, and finding a willing, albeit reluctant, white person to sell them land and help them build a house, especially seeing how easy it was in the North for property to disappear from our hands, if it even got in our hands at all.

This is the kind of faith I'm talking about when it comes to defying gentrification. It's leaning on the strength, witness, and desires of those elders to defy segregation, sharecropping, and lack of resources to have something of their own.

Even if you grew up as part of the migrations out of the South and you're sitting now on a property tax bill on a house that someone is telling you should sell for over a million dollars, you have to have faith that it is still worth it to wait for the right person, who will honor the legacy and the current struggles of a Black American family.

To make it so that even if nobody wants to live there full-time, someone else can, and there's somewhere where y'all can gather as a family.

Or our diaspora of siblings globally trying to find the right place to go, when a homeland feels elusive and stolen.

I had to draw on faith writing up this workbook, because voices are telling me that nobody cares about inner cities. Nobody wants to have farmland. We all gon' just die anyway, so why bother?

But, Spirit laid it on my heart to tell my story. And not just tell my story, but help you shape and tell your land stewardship story as well. I thought this was just going to be an urbanist journey, but my faith walk has turned this into a journey of being the absolute best steward of the Earth that we've been given. The only Earth we've been given.

I hope you'll take this journey of faith with me, because I believe in your contribution to the Earth! And I believe in our ancestors looking down, guiding us to the next step of stewarding the land and Earth.

Trust me, my Dad is totally reading this paragraph right now from the ancestor portal, knowing that the maps he gave me are providing the perfect platform to help me create a map for you right now.

Thing I Can Do 2:
I can create and cultivate

I had to touch the goat's hair. After all, I couldn't believe how silky and curly it was.

If you told five-year-old Kristen, who couldn't wait to get out of rural Rock Creek, North Carolina, and back to the relative urbanity of her Greensboro home, complete with Nickelodeon on repeat and my board games and stuffed animals, that here I was, at the Shenandoah Valley Fiber Festival in Clarke County, Virginia, considering buying a goat, for fiber, she would screech in horror.

And yes, screech. Ask my mom. She still gets chills when I wail at a loud volume.

But this goat. A goat that smells exactly like you'd expect, but not as bad as those old kerosene heaters that I permanently associate with the smell of the country, along with dirt and mothballs.

But, in my 13 years of being a professional fan of cities and all my years of childhood and adulthood leading up to this point, I realized over time that it all boils down to land.

Access to land or, at the very least, access to the raw goods that it produces.

So, I'm a Black, feminine-socialized-and-leaning person from the (so-called) US Southeast. We've established this. I can cook, but I cook for survival.

But when it comes to textiles and fiber… if I needed to be designated as a provider of a particular survival skill if the world as we know it ends and we need civilization to reboot, sign me up for the clothing procurement and production.

Hence, Les and I ended up petting that goat at the 2021 Shenandoah Valley Fiber Festival and considering cleaning up our bathroom in our one-bedroom apartment in Prince George's County, Maryland. Oxon Hill, for those of you who really know, Glassmanor, if you really want to get specific.

And those of you who know the specifics know we have no business whatsoever trying to raise a goat in one of those apartments. Not even the row houses, where the yard would have been doable. The apartments. In our only tub.

So, I resigned myself to just going to the Maryland Sheep and Wool Festival the next spring and getting some fiber already shaved down from a sheep in the fiber barn.

That nice lady, bless her heart, basically turned me off of processing even raw fiber. There was all this talk about taking a washing machine, putting the raw fiber in it after filling it up with water, turning it off, and letting it soak, then scraping the pieces out, and then combing and carding, and spinning it.

That sounds complicated enough, but we didn't have our own washing machine then. This would have had to happen in the laundromat on our basement level. In all the years I shared that apartment with Les, I never went down there, and she went down there if she had a load she could easily do in one swoop.

Plus, the laundromats I have gone to don't seem conducive to washing raw fiber. Most only have side loaders, like we have in our new apartment. And, it costs money to cut on a washing machine in a laundromat. What if I didn't do the rinse setting right? That's literally dollars down the drain.

And yes, as I mentioned before, we have in-unit laundry now. And our first apartment back downtown only had a shower, not a bathtub. Still, the Strucket exists now, and it exists for a reason. Only I want to bathe in our bathtub with my wife. Maybe we'll bathe a future pet cat.

All of this digression gets me to my next point, that defying gentrification takes us being resourceful and getting access to raw materials for ourselves.

The day in 2019 I discovered the crochet class at the DC Public Library, I couldn't get out of my Park View row house and onto the Metro train to get to the cross-town Capitol View branch of the library fast enough.

I had just bought myself a teach myself to crochet kit, procured on Christmas of 2018 after a frantic search to find somewhere in Greensboro to cash my DC check. The JoAnn and the Harris Teeter next to Planet Fitness on West Market Street was my ticket to Christmas that year. (RIP to both!)

I still went back to my mom's, where I worked on my tabletop loom project that night.

But that March morning, I made it to the temporary Capitol View Library in DC, and those nice Black elders helped me finish my scarf, sparking a new movement.
A movement where I could do the crafts of my elders and ancestors, and learn how to control even more means of my production. It's what's given me the courage to design and publish this first edition of this book myself.

And it's got me in some snazzy outfits, both crocheted and sewn.

I've made friends who don't care if I drove there or not, but they also take turns driving and taking Metro.

And I have something that can soothe my soul, from those who continue to insist on having a civic inferiority complex.

What's this about a civic inferiority complex?

It's when you think another city has got it better than yours.

And it might be true in some aspects, like civil rights and job opportunities that pay living wages.

However, in the last decade of living away from my hometown and watching the Internet keep us all connected across borders, I've realized that the arts and crafts I was exposed to as a child make a wonderful gumbo with the go-go that I still hear on DC street corners.

The sound of my accent is its own music.

And siblings, let's never let anyone tell us, especially Black folks in the diaspora, that our cultures aren't worth anything again, while taking our resources out the proverbial back door.

When people think they control your access to resources (or when you think they do), your power is stripped.

And this is how we defy gentrification in spirit and truth, a.k.a the works of our minds and hands.

But let us not forget to care for ourselves as we care for and cultivate our culture.

Thing I Can Do 3:
I can practice self-care

You can't self-care your way out of gentrification. But you can self-care your way through it. This is the ultimate defiance of gentrification.

Because you can be at a rooftop party and it will still rear its ugly head.

I didn't come to the rooftop party to break a plate.

I didn't come to the rooftop party to shake a fence.

I didn't even come to the party with a chip on my shoulder.

And I certainly never imagined that I would be laid up on the ground over five years later, on another side of town, with a slightly different vibe, but still in the same kind of rage over the same kind of violation of what I feel it means to make real community in this town.

After I'd just made a badass speech.

After I'd made multiple attempts to just self-care it all away.

Let me go back and tell you how the anger first started.

As I mentioned before, I met my now wife Les, and on our first few dates back in 2018, she told me about how certain people in the urbanism space were mistreating her.

Giving her foul looks over her appearance.

Correcting her words.

Cutting her out of pictures for environmental organizations because she was too "diverse."

Acting like her neighborhood was the worst in the world, despite being interested in the grittiness of other neighborhoods.

And yes, this triggered the shit out of me.
Around that 2018-2019 period, I hadn't really been talking about how I started the platform. I was getting sick of telling the story about how my Dad had to pee on the side of the road in Greensboro because there were no public bathrooms.
And another story from those same sides of the road, on how he was practically walking in ditches because Greensboro's sidewalk network was raggedy and inconsistent. And that he was walking in the first place because our bus system only picked up people once an hour, if that, and not every day of the week.

Oh, and let's not get into how he became an ancestor. Back when he first died in 2013, I was forgiving and excited to have him to pray to. Now, I rage in grief that he can't just be here making things happen and building an even stronger legacy before he went to the ancestor portal.

And I was so damn tired of telling these stories, where there's no happy ending, and I was starting to exhibit some of his same mental health symptoms, like those bursts of anger, in public.

I'd pivoted to trying to find my voice and stake my claim on the legacy online blogs of urbanism, while positioning The Black

Urbanist in that canon. I even got some mainstream bylines and press.

I realize those spaces were hella white, and they would never be able to hold me down. If anything, they stole my peace with me trying to fit in.

And my home state of North Carolina was gentrifying after all, which is what I was railing about the most on these blogs and such, post losing my Dad. At least they were treating me like the expert I am about these things. But what good is it to be an expert, when the expert checks, if they even write a check, don't pay the rent.

But, as a Black southern millennial, I have no problems bucking up and clapping back to white folks, especially professionally, in such a way that folks don't realize that my expression of "bless your heart," was exactly as passive-aggressive as they expected.

Oh, and code-switching? We don't know her. (I've been one of Mariah Carey's lambs since childhood).

What we do know is that the rent is too damn high, and the jobs don't pay enough, and they expect me to put on a happy Black woman mask and a neurotypical mask, while still sometimes supporting me being a feminist, queer, urbanist.

That's not enough, that's not right, and that's why, in my self-care, I also rage.

Back now to that late April night of 2019 on that rooftop, where the goal was connection, not anger, with other DC urbanists.

But the first match was struck as I, Les, and one of her best friends began to ascend the staircase up to the roof of the condo building in Dupont Circle.

As we climbed up the stairs, a white man in a suit looked down at us.

Six years removed from this situation, I want to give him the benefit of the doubt that, since he was walking down and we were walking up, and the staircase was narrow, he was just making sure that we weren't going to bump into each other or fall backwards into the extremely dark and narrow corridor.

I've even met and mingled and worked with this man since that moment, and he works on Capitol Hill in a prominent position, therefore needs to wear suits to keep his job.

The self-care I practice allows for this kind of individual forgiveness, because I know it opens up my mind for inner peace. I don't forget, though.

Because, even with me giving him the benefit of the doubt now, the weight of the system we live and work in struck a match of anger that would culminate in breaking a plate in the face of one friend and shaking a fence so I wouldn't hurt anyone else.

"I can't take it anymore, I can't take it anymore!"

I screamed as I shook the fence, after knowing that if I really said what I wanted to say, this group of mostly white people would have disowned me on the spot. Many did. Many more would keep their distance over the next few years, and it would birth in me a new kind of rage.

A rage that nearly kept me from writing this book.

A rage that reared up again one night in September 2024.

I'd already been dealing with clapback every time I put out a newsletter, especially after Les returned to being in the transportation and planning industry full-time in 2021.

One of the things I need is praise, audible praise. Thanks, late-diagnosed, but always in the background, autism.

Otherwise, I can't even get out of bed in the morning, much less get on my laptop and write out words that might have some over-concerned Black elder calling my wife within the hour with "concern".

Never praise, all concern.

Concern that got me put off and away from several of the world's favorite urbanist sites, organizations, and collectives, even though it's not like they didn't need to hear the news.

But it's self-care, and the night I'm about to tell you about that's got me back on the keyboard. That way, you can get this game so you don't have to live in this kind of eloquent urbanist rage (shout-out to my fellow Black fiber enthusiast feminist scholar Dr. Brittany Cooper), or if you do, you can know for sure that it's righteous, holy, and exactly what we need to be in right relationship with the one Earth we've been given.

Let me set this scene. It's such a steamy late summer night and we're all trying our best to keep the political timeline that did happen in 2025 from happening.

I can't tell you how much I adore DC's metrobar. Finally, I could kick back and enjoy how cool it is to have a fruity cocktail in a converted mid-century modern metro car, without necessarily needing to explain the mechanics of how the Metro car was decommissioned and moved into the parking lot next to the Rhode Island Avenue-Brentwood station.

I could cool out in that car and be my cute Black, nerdy, queer, neurosparkly, and slightly overheating self.

And that night, September 12, I was there standing on business.

As I said before, I gave a speech from the heart, rallying the mostly white, but also mostly not paying attention, crowd about why the Harris-Walz ticket wasn't perfect, but it was the best option at the moment. Oh, and free us from all the empires and their genocides; Palestine is only just the beginning of that kind of injustice. Oh, and treat Black women like me like you got some sense when you see them at work.

And things were ok when I came off the proverbial stage.

However, I didn't eat before I spoke. I was dehydrated.

Les was hungry, and she wanted to be at the National Black Justice Coalition's Out on the Hill happy hour and another fundraiser for a Black masculine-of-center lesbian's political campaign because for Black politicos and activists, I was *supposed* to be at Congressional Black Caucus (CBC) Week activities that night.

I was honestly upset that there were so many events pulling against me that night. I was missing out on time with a fellow Black nonbinary femme disabled colleague, Victoria Kirby-York,

I'm still processing how classist, ableist, and yes, scared the DC professional and political Black and queer rooms can be, and being able to see one of my comrades that gets me would have been great. But, in true DC form, everything is always going on all at once, and folks with multiple intersections like myself are driven to burnout and rage, having to choose.

Then there's the issue of my white cis male ex, who works in the transportation industry too, and a seemingly Zionist friend of his that decided to come and convince me that we were losing the election over Palestine. And another concerned sista friend who sent me over the edge while meaning well about how much I was sharing with new disabled friends, even though that's what we do to build solidarity across accommodations.

Then poor Les forgot to tell me that the fish joint in the food hall next door was closed, and the taco joint was the only one open when she tried to fix our food problem. All she sent me was a picture of the menu, with no context.

Plus, my ex irritates her, and I thought she ran off and took Metro home to calm down from her own meltdown induced by my also autistic ex.

Even though she came back with some amazing birria tacos, I was already loose and melted down.

I let it all go in audible and violent screams in that metrobar parking lot.

All the fear of the eviction from the spectacular DC apartment that's a dream home that's looming as I put these words on paper, but was only being imagined back then.

Fear that Les would get fired because she could never perform at the level of the performance plan she was just put under, and rage from the future of how she's had to take a pay cut and walk away just to save her own mental health and life.

Fear that this election cycle would end up as it did, and now we are under surveillance and occupation.

Fear that I would forever have to crochet and color and never get back to making a single dime, telling you that you could defy gentrification.

About 30 minutes later, I lay on that ground next to the metrobar pylon that doubles as the restrooms, head pounding, vision blurred, yielding up to law enforcement, not because I wanted to, but because I was expecting my fate to be decided by the state and its most violent forces, because I'd had enough and I dared to say it again in front of all the "wrong" people and at the "wrong" place.

Because, guess what. I can only self-care myself, but so far.

Without the community meeting me in the middle, I can't defy gentrification.

Again, we have to do this together.

Through self-care as a political act. With tools that aren't the masters.

And if we share identity markers, you can take a deep breath, turn the page, and listen, and maybe even read along as I let everyone have it.

Because again, this is eloquent rage, and yes, this is self-care too.

(Or if you just want to work on solutions together, go to page 71)

Everybody else, get those tissues ready, you get to cry your white tears, but you don't get to walk away and claim that you didn't do anything wrong.

Part 2:
The Things I Need From You

Thing I need from you 1:
Community care

You gotta give a fuck about us. Yes, I cussed. I can't express it any nicer. After all, y'all think you're being nice when you tell us we need to do X, Y, and Z to be upstanding citizens of cities.

No, we don't. We are beings that live on the Earth. We have cometogether in an urbanization. Urbanization is not the sole domain of the rich, famous, or "together."

Hence why instead of a cute story, this chapter's gon' feel a little preachy, but we need some motivation, if all that work we just did is going to happen.

And if you're not the target audience of the first three chapters, we need your support.

People often see me on the Internet, ranting and raving about how I think this company is shady and how I don't do certain things.

When you care about people from your own heart, my criticism shouldn't hit so hard.

When I teased this workbook, I wrote the following list of things people wanted me to do to "defy gentrification:"

— **Get a minority supplier certification**, so I can be a sub (and only a sub) contractor on a project plan that may never come to fruition, leaving more people without transit and homeless, TODAY, when the rent is due and the sheriff is sitting outside of the door, and the job requires you to clock in with your fingers at 8:00 a.m. sharp, even though your bus was a ghost after all.

— **Forget about said people because the Lord has blessed me to be in this home, and to be in rooms with high people, so I should close the door behind me**. (I noted in the original text that if I had done this, folks wouldn't even know the names of some solid urbanists!)

— Speaking of those urbanists, **we should all stop wasting time on calling out and dismantling food insecurity, homelessness, public health crises, colonialism, and warmongering, because urbanism is just transportation, luxury apartments, and fancy stores, hotels, and restaurants in mixed-use configurations**.

So, let me break these down, as these three bullets illustrate what I mean by y'all needing to care about us.

First, unless you are putting your "minority" subcontractors on a shelf (and you think that they are minorities in the first place), then that part isn't about you.

But, if that's you: Yeah, you deserve every bit of shaking in your bones and shifting in your seat, along with the watering of eyes that's happening to you reading this.

Talk to your other colleagues who have come out on the other side of feeling that level of discomfort. Let them tell you how much of a gift it is to have a diverse staff. That inclusion is what's kept them in business because they have a justification to say they belong in the communities they are in. It's not a slight to them when they get ready to extend partnerships and share wealth with community members and leaders, modeling spacial restorative justice.

Stop barking at people because you're scared. If you can't find it in you to care about the people you're serving, nor serve the people you can't stop seeing as tenants, community nuisances, and sadly, criminals, then get out of this field.

The era of the oligarchs will only last as long as people aren't wise to what they are doing and people don't have knowledge of their power. The internet can't be completely destroyed.

Secondly, speaking of higher powers, and leaning into my Black church roots, the God I grew up being told to serve and fear, sent his child, whom we do gender as male, but that could be flexible, according to the legend, to challenge the empire.

The birth was miraculous, the miracles were controversial, and he (we're going to go with he in this paragraph) willingly died as a criminal of the empire, but then came back to life to show that he was beyond the empire.

Yet, so many of us affiliated with the Black church can't accept that Jesus, the one that we are so happy to sic on someone who is supposedly sinning, wants us to honor and serve.

That he wouldn't want us to let people be hungry and without shelter. He even said that there would come a time when we wouldn't worship him in the place they were standing in (you might know this place as the contested, but rightful land of Palestinians, of all faiths), but in spirit and in truth.

Not at a church, mosque, synagogue, or even a temple or altar, but in our minds and our words.

So, especially if you claim to be tapping into a form of the divine for your work and life, you are called upon to make sure that people are ok, because after all, because of their sacrifice and despite our knowledge of it, we are all holy and divine.

But then I know some of y'all don't believe that and love your regimented religion. So then again, stop acting like you care, because you don't. But you need to.

Finally, I wouldn't be writing this book if I didn't love my high-rise apartment, the DC Metro (and other Metros, flaws and all), libraries, and having my childhood grocery store in walking distance, despite the fact that they thought they could gentrify me out of their customer base.

But, you, my friend with the map crayon in hand, you can't expect your drawings to be real without thinking about the people using those things you're drawing.

Some things should stay on crayons and paper, with maybe a touch of clay and papier mâché if you want to make a slightly more realistic map of your fake place.

On the flip side, having those crayons and papier mâché as your only tools and social media as your only voice doesn't mean you don't care. After all, what kind of hypocritical workbook would this be?

I've encouraged my siblings in the faith chapter earlier in this workbook to have faith, in their vision, in their dreams, in the work they just did.

And I have faith, allies and accomplices, that you can do the same.

Thing I need from you 2:
Infrastructure

This entire blogging, social media, and writing platform exists because I simply wanted rail transit in my hometown of Greensboro, North Carolina.

I wrote my first blog post about this in 2009 on a blog site powered by Google's Blogspot I called Waxing Philosophical. It was supposed to be my bridge between writing on Xanga, an early 2000s blogging platform that tended to lean towards the personal and the religious, and being marketable for more journalism, public relations, and marketing jobs than the ones I had in campus communications as an NC State undergraduate.

Xanga, was not as popular as LiveJournal, but the vibes were very similar. Personal essays and journals, that could magically be read and commented on.

For nerdy, neurodivergent, closeted children, teens, and young adults of the late 1990s and early 2000s, this, along with sites like BlackPlanet, created that feeling of community that we thought Facebook and Twitter were going to just exponentially expand and enhance our culture.. Something exponentially happened, but it's not all been good.

In fact, so many of your favorite journalists, influencers, and online entrepreneurs started right here on that Internet, despite Xanga going defunct in the early 2010s and technically becoming a WordPress site, and LiveJournal, which I never used, going somewhere else. It's why we love Substack so much, because it takes us back to that era, where so many of us who are lovers of typing a lot of words thrive.

Those early years of the World Wide Web coincided with my years in grade school. America Online and Prodigy were deemed too expensive by my family, despite their promises on the copious CD-ROMs that were mailed to our homes alongside music CD offers from Columbia House and BMG.

However, a used Macintosh Classic II, an email address from Mindspring, and permission to access Nickelodeon.com, disney.com, and one other child-friendly site were absolutely within our budget. I also loved playing with the preloaded games, several of which were just like the ones I adored in the school's computer lab.

Fast forward to that 2009 blog post. I got to the point where I thought I could change offline infrastructure with a click because of this access to online infrastructure and the care and concern of my family and my school community to make sure I had early access to computers, the Internet, and creativity.

I'd specifically like to thank Oregon Trail, PrintShop, and my uncle Phil, who was our family tech expert for so long, for nurturing those seeds.

I've since learned that there are a few more steps one needs to change offline infrastructure, but what I want y'all to know in this chapter is that providing that infrastructure makes all the difference for someone like me to be a person and not just a worker, student, or citizen.

I know we worry about the cost of healthcare and transit, but having those two things at no or low cost, at least on my end, helps me continue to create.

How many people do we not know or have lost, because they couldn't get anywhere, especially to health care, in enough time?

Think especially about how many of those people are Black, queer, disabled, and low-resource. I would call the fourth group poor with no problem, but in this case, are they really poor, or are you just denying them resources?

If we want a world where having multiple cultures is a benefit and love is infinite, we have to provide the infrastructure.

As you see with me, it pays off!

Thing I need from you 3:
Access

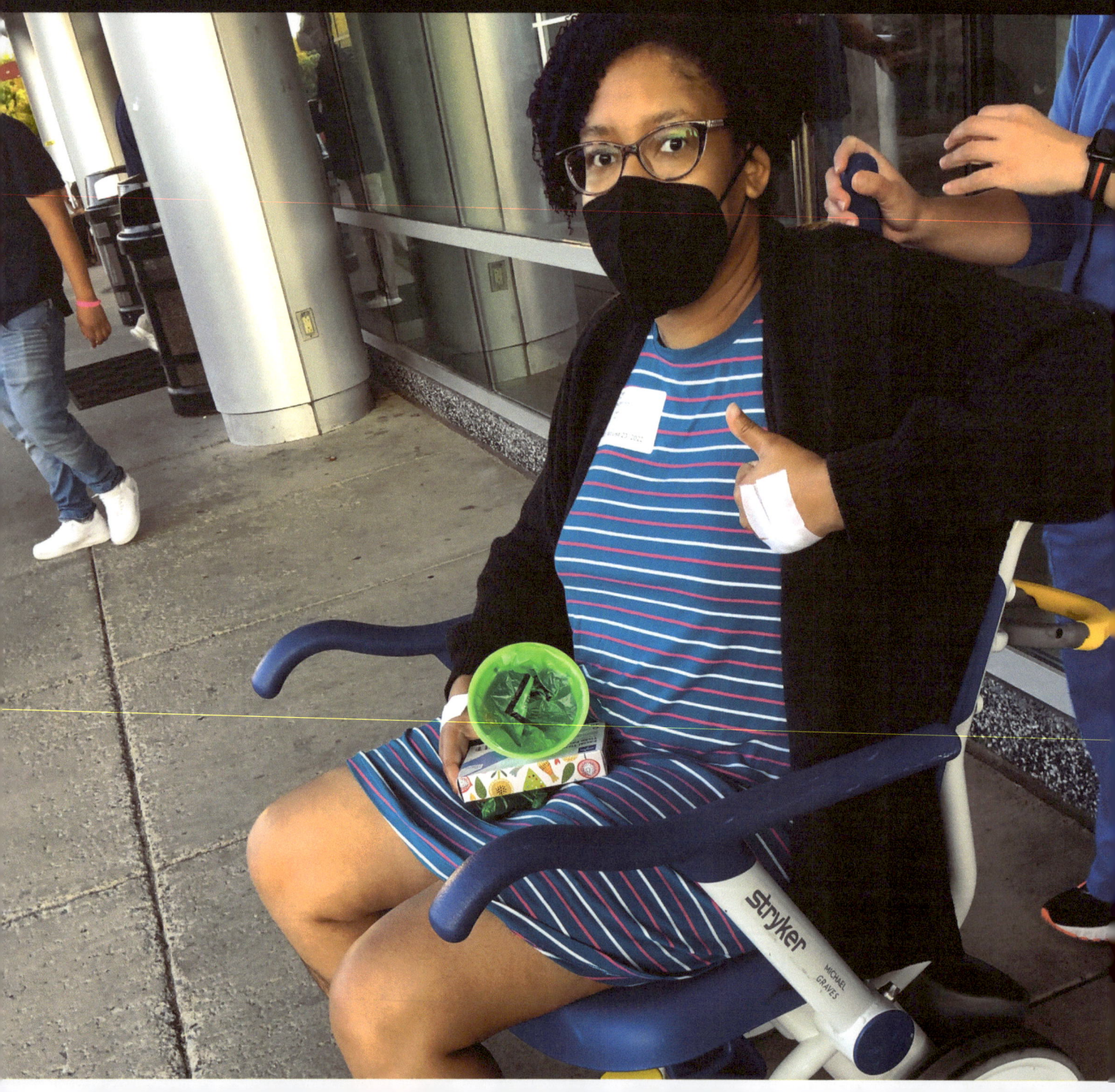

Caring means that we have access.
Access to homes.
Access to community spaces.
Access to income.
Get that concrete pouring and ready for the ramps.
Get those teachers and support staff hired for the schools and community centers.

Back in May of 2023, when I received the email that our apartment building was seeking tenants in our income range, and all we needed to do was tour the apartment and submit our financial documents for verification, I immediately stopped everything I was doing and scheduled an appointment.

I made sure I wore one of the outfits that still looks nice and still fits after my pandemic weight gain. Yes, I know discrimination based on appearance is illegal on paper, but it's alive and well in real life, and it costs a lot of money to prove.

Speaking of proving and approvals, when the approval papers for our apartment came back weeks later, Les and I still couldn't believe that we were actually approved for this apartment in the luxury building on the Wharf.

We looked at other houses for sale. We got rejected by AI for an apartment in an equally nice building in Prince George's County, but near Metro's New Carrollton station on the Orange Line. We considered buying all of our new furniture and just putting it in the Glassmanor apartment. New furniture would absolutely fit, unlike our proverbial goat from the cultivation section.

But, what I kept coming back to is Les's vision for what her DC life would look like. My vision for my DC life has always been a little less specific around where I would live, besides a Wardman row house and using said row house to create community in a place that's hellbent on devoiding itself of it.

Hers was clear. Living in an apartment in Navy Yard or the Wharf near the water. Having a Green Line commute to a job in community outreach for transportation. Having adequate access to health care.

So many people have similar visions. What they don't have is similar access.

We can enjoy our apartment, even if we start having trouble using our legs, and so can our friends and family with mobility issues.

I still run an air purifier and use nasal sprays, mouthwash, and mask with an N95 respirator in common areas to not just combat multiple infections of COVID, but my lifelong issues with my sinuses, and my new post-COVID issues with my stomach.

Honestly, I can tell we have better air filters, along with cleaner appliances and floors from the start.

I know folks hate how these new apartments have no overhead lighting, but when I'm in sensory overload, it's so clutch that these rooms go completely dark and I can just chill with a night light!

Plus, being near water and being able to walk outside without the threat of catcalling being all present (it's still there, just mixed up with all kinds of other people), allows me to access dreams I thought were dead.

You, as the real estate provider, urban planner, elected or appointed official, or even just an employer or funder providing the capital for our vision, can spare those extra dollars you think providing something like inclusionary zoning takes away from you.

You as the employer, can set a salary floor and work with your employees, not pay them so little that when they think about their situation, it resembles a sharecropping arrangement, sadly, without the housing, so it resembles something even worse.

Our class (and race) integrated building adds back that community element and makes it so people create new ideas that come with their own currency.

Let me remind you again that the next step of caring is access. But I have one last request of you in the next section.

Thing I need from you 4:
Convenience

Just like we have a certain association with faith, the one we have with convenience also looks a certain way.

It looks like dingy fluorescent lights and stale hot dog orders. It might include rotten foods and a mean cat, meaner than the man behind the counter, encased in glass, who demands that you walk straight to the counter or else.

We, unfortunately have seen what that or else looks like on a global scale, in the snuffed-out lives of George Floyd and Alton Sterling, along with so many other people of all genders, in stories that barely get any local coverage.

Yet the grief is there. And, you're pushing the limits of that eleventh hour, as you're slipping closer to the seventh-hour, in the middle of the night, hoping to find sustenance for yourself.

You get home and look in the mirror again, and of course, the world tells you that you shouldn't be this fat and that your children deserve to get taken away tomorrow, because you can't find work close enough and their school hates them, but it's right down the street and you're supposed to send them there.

Because it's convenient. Oh, and the bus is an hour late. So much for convenience.

However, like everything else, they try to make us as Black folks ashamed for desiring and wanting, convenience is not a sin, nor is it a shame.

When I experience convenience at the moment, it's in my 200+ resident apartment building, which is convenient to the DC Southwest Waterfront. Restaurants and shops of all kinds line it, and I get to walk or roll out of my building and down the sidewalk, the bike lane, or the cobblestone street to all of them.

If I follow the sidewalk in the other direction, I can be on any Metrorail line I want, within 15 minutes, or I can step right outside of the door, go around the corner, and there's an e-bike or a Metrobus that will ferry me where I need to go.

A full-service Safeway is just on the other side of the regional award-winning theater, Arena Stage, that's putting on even more Black art performances, including the one Les and I got married during in June 2025. I can hop on the bus and I can get off in five minutes to a solid Whole Foods, that can handle my odd dietary needs, and a Harris Teeter that looks just like it does in North Carolina, in case I need a convenient way to eat myself out of my homesickness.

Oh, and I can't forget my new grocery boo, Wegmans, which is now just off the Yellow Line and next to the sister in her own luxury salon suite who makes my hair all kinds of glorious, respectably defying shades of blue and purple and pink. We did peacock for the wedding, and I love it!

I can just walk to a newly renovated Southwest Library, where I can get all the many benefits of DC Public Libraries and their mission to be a third place for everyone in our community.

I can walk to pray and meditate in neighboring buildings that have Pride flags in the windows.

When I get back home, I'm greeted by the nicest concierges. My packages are either in our package locker or their room. I fob up on our elevator, knowing only my fellow residents, many of whom are also Black, of all economic classes, are also benefiting from having this space.

The apartment is bright, airy, free of mold, and we have the best couch and bed one could ask for. I grab my crochet hooks, turn on some YouTube or an audiobook, and chill out, making as many of my clothes as possible.

Defining convenience for ourselves is the third key to this pursuit of defying gentrification.

Everyone should have buildings and townhouse blocks that are full of all kinds of people. Housing and eating shouldn't depend on how much we can labor. After all, I've found that people find something to do when they are given their basic needs. Public transportation should be available and efficient at no cost to the poorest. Supermarkets, schools, arts institutions, libraries, and other institutions should be numerous.

And, by the time you hold this book, I will have moved on from this apartment. and used the manifesto to ask the community for convenience, trusting that there's a community on the other side that wants to do that for me. And it is, because humans, naturally, when nurtured, want to help each other.

This is why I say that defying gentrification, in the pursuit of destroying gentrification, is a group project.

Let's roll up our sleeves and get to work for our communities of convenience.

Part 3
The Work (Book) We All Need To Do

In this section, you'll find all the worksheets you need to help you take action on what you've read in prior sections.

Depending on how you've read the book, you'll answer these questions and do these exercises as someone who needs relief from gentrification or someone who needs to release it as a way of being and doing business. You may need to do a little bit of both, but please keep in mind your privileges and positions in your daily life and in society as a whole. Please don't just do this once and never look at it again. In fact, reviewing these sections will help you with your own personal growth.

I've made a digital version of this, which you can access by scanning the QR code below or typing in **http://bit.ly/4gYGlN2**, where you can share with me what your specific playbook is and get real-time updates on what others are finding out about themselves and their community through this process. I've also put a link there to my living syllabus of references!

THE BASICS WORKSHEET

This is the worksheet where you take inventory of what you do have in the place you live. If you aren't able to check a box, keep that in mind as you go through the next sections and rank and rate where you live. And I left some blank, to add your own. Feel free to do this here, or scan the QR code to access the digital version on Typeform.

Does It Have?	Yes	No	Optional: What Does it Cost For You
Housing Affordable to Your Budget			
Housing in the Aesthetic Style You Want			
Housing Large Enough for Your Core Family			
Housing Near Transit			
A Hospital or Clinic that takes your insurance and is available 24/7			
24-hour Public Transit			
12-16 hour public transit			
Free public transit			
A place where you can make income			
A school that affirms and welcomes your children			
Grocery stores near transit or in walking distance			

Does It Have?	Yes	No	Optional: What Does it Cost For You
A university or lifelong learning center that affirms you			
A place where you can make income that is accessible to public transit			
A library without banned books and with other resources			

WHAT WILL IT TAKE FOR YOU TO DEFY AND DISMANTLE GENTRIFICATION WORKSHEET?

This worksheet goes deeper into how to pinpoint what a specific metro area has and how it can work for you, as someone who has my exact intersectional identity, someone who might be a little more privileged, or someone who is a complete ally, or someone who needs to actively dismantle a terrible environment or system. Yes, well well-meaning landlord, that's you!

So I start each section of this worksheet with what I require for each space I mention, questions to ask yourself on your personal journey to that kind of space, questions to guide allyship and solidarity for having that kind of space in your community, and what tasks need to be undertaken to facilitate justice, access, and belonging.

I've been working on or with a version of this worksheet since 2018, when CityLab produced an evaluation of what they thought Black women (and only women, no acknowledgment of gender diversity), would need in a metro area.
The analysis assumed that we would just need jobs, good schools, and hospitals, and we could then pay market-rent or obtain a mortgage on any property we wanted. That we could go into any business. That we would even want to use traditional hospitals or higher education. Because that survey left so much out, I drew up another one that used similar questions. Scan the QR Code on page 51 you can use these questions as they are written out here and write them in your own journal.

Also, head to page 64 where I share the principles of Black Queer Feminist Urbanism.

If you are using this section to help you heal and build despite not having adequate versions of any of this, after reading each set of prompts, I would suggest doing the full suite of CliftonStrengths analysis on yourself, as I think they are an amazing way to see what the white, neurotypical world thinks your strengths are, while not harping on your "weaknesses".

Creative Spaces

Kristen's Requirement:
Artist and makerspaces, materials suppliers, funding, and communities that are inclusive of Black people and Black cultural and art products.

Questions to Guide Your Personal Journey:
I put this one first because I have found this one to be a measure of how much Black joy is available in a metro area and how it's respected. What arts and cultural spaces do you need to be able to consume on a regular basis? What arts and cultural practices do you need to be able to practice/make on a regular basis?

Questions to Guide Your Solidarity:
What arts and cultural spaces do your friends and colleagues, especially those who identify as Black, queer, feminist, poor/broke, and/or disabled and who depend on public transportation, have access to consistently and in a budget-friendly manner?

What steps/actions can you take to facilitate justice, access, and belonging in this area?

Business Environments

Kristen's Requirement:
Workplaces of all kinds, that pay and fund fairly, that are inclusive and respectful of all gender presentations and sexualities of Black people.

Questions to Guide Your Personal Journeys:
What do you need in a place of work and/or entrepreneurial support circle? Do you need or want to continue working for the same employer? Do you want to work for yourself? When do you want to gain financial independence? When do you want to retire?

Questions to Guide Your Solidarity:
Are Black folks of any gender and income/work level treated well in your office? Who has power in your office, and how does that power treat you versus how they may treat Black folks of any gender? If you have a Black supervisor, does that relationship affirm you or make you uncomfortable?

What steps/actions can you take to facilitate justice, access, and belonging in this area?

Non-Medical Hair/Body Care

Kristen's Requirement:
Hair and beauty salons that love and affirm the way our hair comes out of our heads, that are also priced fairly and clearly, and centrally located to transit and/or amenities.

Questions to Guide Your Personal Journey:
How do you like to wear your hair? Do you feel like you have the support you need to wear it like that? Is that support centrally located or even available where you live? Is it within your budget?

Questions to Guide Your Allyship:
Do hair and beauty providers provide services for non-White people? Do they force certain procedures on their hair if they do service them -- like chemical relaxers and flat ironing? Have you mocked Black folks, especially women and gender non-conforming and/or trans folks for how they've decided to wear their hair? Have you brought up professionalism standards against them for their hair choices? If you do notice black hair providers, are they positioned near transit?

What steps/actions can you take to facilitate justice, access, and belonging in this area?

Food

Kristen's Requirement:
A solid mixture of food from other ethnicities and North-Carolina style soul food that I can at least be driven to or take transit to, especially when I need to find comfort in said food.

Questions to Guide Your Personal Journey:
What dietary needs do you have? What kind of access to cultural foods do you need? Do you need a variety of cuisines? Do they have to be prepared? Do you need certain items stocked at the grocery store? Do you need to be near a grocery store?

Questions to Guide Your Allyship:
Are there a variety of food cultures in close proximity to public transportation, functional sidewalks, and walking trails? If a colleague or friend is in need of a particular foodway to honor their culture, were you able to aid them in finding it or knowing where to find it? Do you respect all foodways, even if you may not personally like the smell, taste, texture, or feel of the foodway?

What steps/actions can you take to facilitate justice, access and belonging in this area?

Spiritual Spaces

Kristen's Requirement:
Houses of faith, that center Afro-Diaspora faith traditions and other indigenous faith traditions, that also affirm queer and trans identities, partnerships, families, and leadership.

Questions to Guide Your Personal Journey:
What do you need in a spiritual space? Do you need a formal spiritual space/community outside of your home? If you choose to make one in your home, what does your home need for that to be created?

Questions to Guide Your Allyship:
Does your spiritual space affirm the spiritual journeys and humanness of all people? Does it do so with clarity and concern about the well-being of the most marginalized outside of its walls? Does it marginalize in its attempt to not marginalize? Are you guilty of marginalizing others through spiritual tactics? Is your spiritual space accessible for those with different abilities and those who use public transportation?

What steps/actions can you take to facilitate justice, access and belonging in this area?

Bookstores and Libraries

Kristen's Requirement:
Centrally-located, staffed, and titled with Black and/or LGBTQIA+ people/authors. Also, lean into their role as community third spaces and cultural producers.

Questions to Guide Your Personal Journey:
Do you need a library or bookstore in close proximity? Do you want to exclusively support Black bookstores or others of marginalized groups?

Questions to Guide Your Allyship:
Even if the bookstore has a specific focus (queer, feminist, Black, AAPI, faith-based), does it help you find books you need, even if that means a referral to another bookstore? Can those who are marginalized find themselves on the bookshelves of the bookstores available to them?

What steps/actions can you take to facilitate justice, access, and belonging in this area?

Natural Resources

Kristen's Requirement:
Indoor and outdoor recreation areas with staff and programming that is Black-friendly and LGBTQIA+-affirming.

Questions to Guide Your Personal Journey:
Do you need to be able to get out into nature? What about an indoor gym/recreational space?

Questions to Guide Your Allyship:
Do the recreational spaces have commitments to telling the full and truthful story of the lands that they are on? Do the gym spaces treat all attendees with dignity and respect?

What steps/actions can you take to facilitate justice, access, and belonging in this area?

Social Affirmation Spaces Not Already Included

Kristen's Requirement:
LGBTQIA+ spaces that aren't just for wealthy, white, cis, or abled queer people. Black spaces that aren't queer-antagonistic, or bougie.

Questions to Guide Your Personal Journey:
What do you need your social spaces to feel like? If you're in a Black service organization, what do you need that to feel and be like? If you are a parent, what kind of parent support do you need? Do you share my need for LGBTQIA+ or global majority spaces to be more inclusive? Do you need spaces amenable to dating? Whatever you need that we haven't already covered, share it here, and we'll talk about it, too.

Questions to Guide Your Allyship:
If you are part of a space for one marginalized identity, is it intersectional? Does it openly believe that only some members of its community are worthy of care and concern? Does it practice respectability politics? Is it available and accessible to all who share the main marginalization?

What steps/actions can you take to facilitate justice, access, and belonging in this area?

THE RAGE PAGE

Honestly, you may just want to use this page to vent and rage about it all. Go ahead sista-sibling. You are heard, you are loved, and here, what you really feel about all of this is ok. But, if you let it all out here and you are ready to work with some of the other pages, then feel free to turn back. However, this page is enough.

If you see yourself as an ally, this is the only page where you can cry your white tears, but I'm going to need you to turn back some pages and do more work.

Conclusion: What's Next

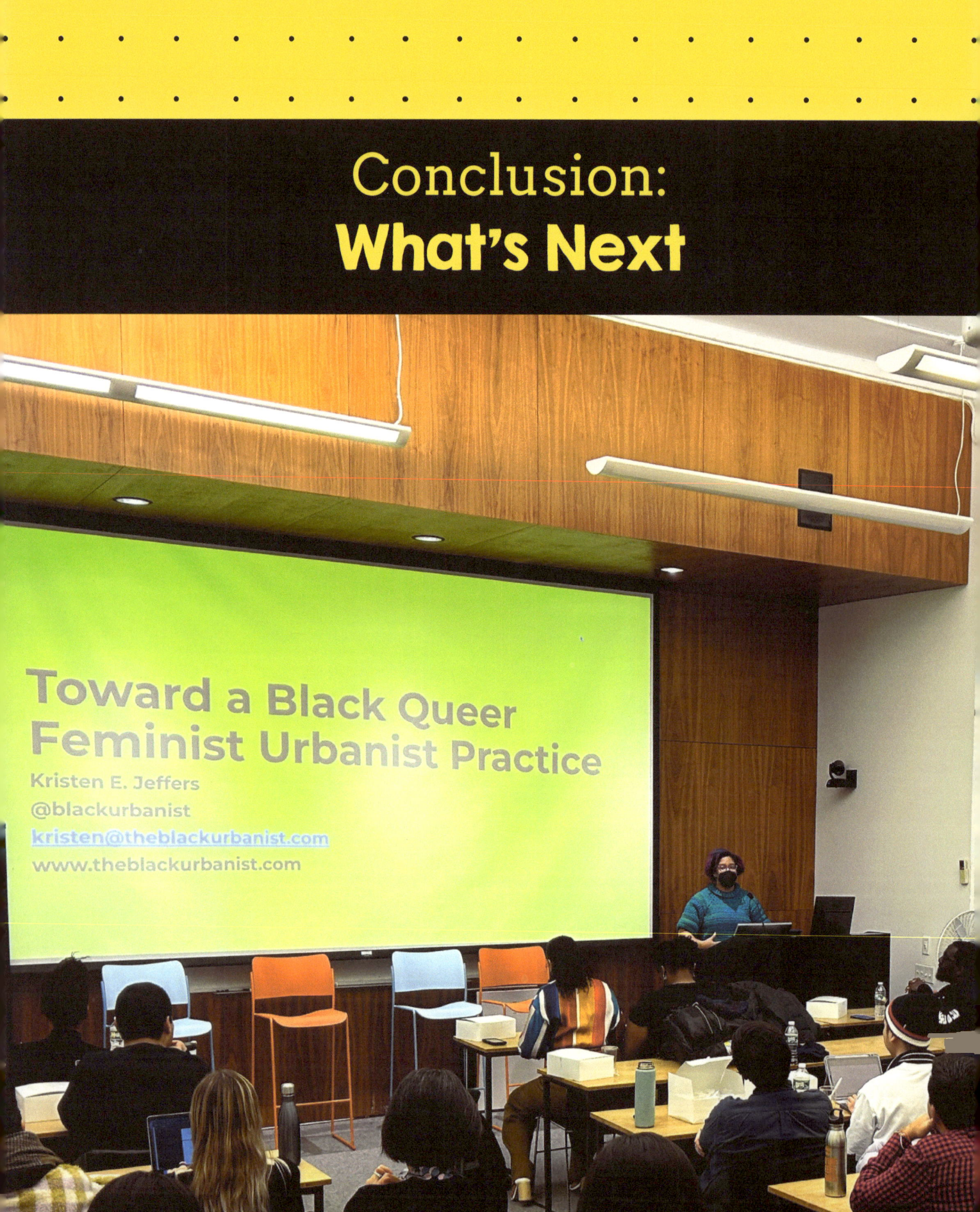

The world can benefit from seeing itself and then acting in a Black Queer Disabled Feminist Urbanist framework, even if that's not exactly who they are.

In this section, I will clarify a few definitions and principles of what I mean by Black Queer Disabled Feminist Urbanist, so that you, no matter how few or many intersections we share, can see, especially after I share the whys, how this exercise of my self-care becomes a practice of community care. Pair this with the Defying Gentrification Manifesto, and you'll be on the same page with how I see us thriving.

Additionally, all of this work was influenced by this quote by Malcolm X in his speech to women in 1964: *The most disrespected person in America is the Black woman. The most un-protected person in America is the Back woman. The most neglected person in America, is the Black woman.*

Sadly, Malcolm X was assassinated before his vision of a more Black feminist, Black Muslim, and American community came to fruition. But I believe that my life and my visions have been given to me to share this vision to help us in these times.

So for clarity, Here are my definitions of Black, Queer, Disabled, Feminist, and Urbanist:

Black: A person of African descent, often with visibly melanated skin, who has been subjected directly or through ancestry to enslavement, colonization, discrimination, or mistreatment as a result of their ethnicity, past and present marginalization, and/or skin color. This also refers to the cultures derived from these activities and their adaptation to their environments.

Queer: A person who has a gender presentation, gender identity, gender journey/relationship, or sexual orientations that differ from traditional Western colonial thoughts on such ideas. Also refers to cultures that develop from this state of being.

Disabled: A person whose body doesn't perform at the speed, function, or other desire of capitalism or white normative society. Yes, in a systemic way, this means bodies that are too fat and too dark are disabled, along with those who are missing limbs, who have brain processing delays or hyperfocus, who have illnesses that keep one from participating in what is deemed appropriate, specifically a workplace with rigid definitions.

Feminist: A person and a movement that honor genders marginalized under patriarchy, traditionally those tagged as feminine or outside traditional gender binaries.

Urbanist: A person and a movement that promotes the conglomeration of ideas, services, and objects in centralized locations, governed democratically, given freely and fairly, and connected by public transit and other people-powered transportation networks such as sidewalks and multi-use bicycle and pedestrian paths. Not mutually exclusive to rural expressions, but the natural output of natural and rural environments that have high levels of human interaction.

These are the definitions I came up with from both tapping into my spiritual journey and from years of academic study, continuing independent education on and offline, and just observing the world around me and listening. Then, as I thought of the specific areas of my needs around Black Queer Disabled Feminist Urbanism, I came up with these "whys" because:

Spiritual Spaces: Our souls are weary and deserve comfort and uplift, in modes that affirm and honor us.

Housing: Shelter and housing are human rights; they should never have been and shouldn't continue to be a commodity.

Transportation: We should never have to worry about how we will navigate this Earth; that's just as much ours as anyone else's.

Food: Our food and foodways should nourish us in abundance.

Health, Wellness, and Caregiving: We deserve to be in good health, practicing communal wellness and wellbeing. Our health, like our shelter, should never be a commodity, outside of fair trade to receive needed supplies and tools to maintain our health.

Work and Finance: In whatever skill or created object we choose to trade with others, we are deserving of that trade or product to be given freely and compensated for fairly. We should never be assumed to be incapable of any task we take on.

Natural Environments and Recreation: We steward this Earth and allow it to nourish and nurture us. We do not actively work against it or destroy it for our gain.

Arts and Cultural Space: Our dreams made manifest deserve to be seen, heard, and shaped, first in equitable measure and later equal measure.

Grooming and Adornment Spaces: Our bodies are beautiful and deserve to be adorned and adored in ways that honor who we really are and the gifts that come from the corners of the Earth we inhabit, no matter what corner of the earth that is.

Identity, Affinity, and Human Rights: We deserve to be, likewise others deserve to be and we should conduct ourselves and honor our innate and natural differences not as a reason to marginalize, but as a necessary part of our human ecosystem.

Education: We are lifelong learners, and everywhere has the potential to be a classroom or a space of knowledge exchange. In addition, we learn from everyone, no matter their age or era.

Now I know you're thinking, aren't these just principles of human rights? Why label them this way? First of all, we need to meet our world where it is, which makes these distinctions between us. Secondly, until the day we are no longer marginalizing or worse, destroying or killing members of these overlapping communities, we need to start our focus here. And yes, all bodies deserve to be in public spaces.

Gentrification, along with its siblings, does nothing but create harm and a lack of value. I promise you can still make money in other places besides someone's house.

You could put up the funds for a community land trust, and then invest in all of the art that comes from the people who no longer have to pay rent to you, or worry about being displaced in the middle of their grand opus or masterpiece.

Your community-focused bank could back up local municipal bonds, which would in turn create transit systems, libraries, hospitals, and other places that create humans that are abundant in creativity and opportunity.

This guide and workbook gives you a custom plan to work with yourself and others to create the places you deserve.

And I can't wait to see what happens when we all live in a world where we honor the divinity and resourcefulness of all of us.

Acknowledgments

If it isn't obvious, besides the Creator, I want to most thank my wife Les Henderson for the encouragement to keep going until I finally wrote a version of this book. She is not only resilient in the face of the struggles I've talked about in this book, she is a beautiful force. I love you babe!

I also want to thank Shawnon Corprew for providing me with developmental editing, copy-editing, and even employment support for a portion of the production of this book. Lacey Anthony and Kate Murdler for being two of the good ones!

Regina Anaejionu for her book training in 2023, which encouraged me to write my story and theories in relation to gentrification. I used to be so afraid of that word, but now, we are slaying this dragon together.

Hannah Oliver Depp of Loyalty Bookstores, L'Oreal Thompson Payton of Zora's Books, and the Youngs of Mahogany Books, for being willing to be some of my first shelvers! Also, thanks to all the published authors and independent booksellers who believed a general audience could benefit from this.

Wannona Satcher and Kevin Hamak for asking about my book, whatever book that it is.

Charles T. Brown for telling us nobody in urbanism cares, and to keep on going.

The LockedIn Substack writers group and the Anacostia Fiber Enthusiasts Collective for providing me with creative outlets and giving me other perspectives.

Dee Powell, Jacob Smith, and all my mentees, past, present, and future, for reminding me that they are here because I am here and that urbanism isn't what it was; it's what we are creating together.

My family and friends, both blood and chosen, living and in the ancestor portal, for your patience and your encouragement, both directly and indirectly.

My medical team who helped me realize it's not all in my head.

And finally, all of you, who saw fit to pick up this book and get something out of it!

About the Author

Kristen Jeffers (she/they) is the creator and managing editor of The Black Urbanist and Kristpattern multimedia platforms, which strive to bring a Black queer feminist, dynamically disabled perspective to the greater urbanist sphere through a newsletter, workbook, and podcast on Defying Gentrification, and facilitating crochet and other needlecraft workshops and spaces. She's held a variety of communication and public affairs positions over the last decade and a half and is one of Planetizen's 2023 100 Most Influential Contemporary Urbanists. Most recently, they were the contributing editor for Greater Greater Washington and have been featured in the New York Times, Washington Post, Streetsblog, the Commercial Appeal, and on NPR affiliates, WAMU, WUNC, and KCUR, along with bylines in House Beautiful, Sierra Magazine, Streetsblog, Next City, and Grist. They live between Washington, DC, Maryland, and North Carolina, with their wife Les Henderson, and were born and raised in Greensboro, NC.

Stay in touch and plug into our movement at www.defyinggentrification.com

www.ingramcontent.com/pod-product-compliance
Lightning Source LLC
Chambersburg PA
CBHW040210100526
44585CB00003BA/110